Janice VanCleave's
VOLCANOES

JANICE VANCLEAVE'S SPECTACULAR SCIENCE PROJECTS

Animals
Earthquakes
Gravity
Machines
Magnets
Microscopes and Magnifying Lenses
Molecules
Volcanoes

JANICE VANCLEAVE'S SCIENCE FOR EVERY KID SERIES

Astronomy for Every Kid
Biology for Every Kid
Chemistry for Every Kid
Earth Science for Every Kid
Geography for Every Kid
Math for Every Kid
Physics for Every Kid

Spectacular Science Projects

Janice VanCleave's
VOLCANOES

Mind-boggling Experiments You Can Turn Into Science Fair Projects

John Wiley & Sons, Inc.
New York • Chichester • Brisbane • Toronto • Singapore

This text is printed on acid-free paper.

Science advisor: Paul J. Kravitz, Bronx High School of Science
Design and Production by Navta Associates, Inc.
Illustrated by Doris Ettlinger

Library of Congress Cataloging-in-Publication Data
VanCleave, Janice Pratt.
   [Volcanoes]
   Janice VanCleave's volcanoes: mind-boggling experiments you can turn into science
fair projects.
   p.   cm. — (Spectacular science projects)
   Includes index.
   ISBN 0-471-30811-0 (acid-free paper)
   1. Volcanoes—Experiments—Juvenile literature. 2. Science projects—Juvenile litera-
ture. [1. Volcanoes—Experiments. 2. Science projects. 3. Experiments.] I. Title. II. Title:
Volcanoes. III. Series: VanCleave, Janice Pratt. Janice VanCleave's spectacular science
projects.
   QE521.3.V376   1994
   551.2'1'078—dc20   93-23148

Printed in the United States
10 9 8 7 5

CONTENTS

This book is dedicated to a very special friend,

David Sobel

Introduction

Science is a search for answers. Science projects are good ways to learn more about science as you search for the answers to specific problems. This book will give you guidance and provide ideas, but you must do your part in the search by planning experiments, finding and recording information related to the problem, and organizing the data collected to find the answer to the problem. Sharing your findings by presenting your project at science fairs will be a rewarding experience if you have properly prepared for the exhibit. Trying to assemble a project overnight results in frustration, and you cheat yourself out of the fun of being a science detective. Solving a scientific mystery, like solving a detective mystery, requires planning and the careful collecting of facts. The following sections provide suggestions for how to get started on this scientific quest. Start the project with curiosity and a desire to learn something new.

SELECT A TOPIC

The 20 topics in this book suggest many possible problems to solve. Each topic has one "cookbook" experiment—follow the recipe and the result is guaranteed. Approximate metric equivalents have been given after all English measurements. Try several or all of these easy experiments before choosing the topic you like best and want to know more about. Regardless of the problem you choose to solve, what you discover will make you more knowledgeable about volcanoes.

KEEP A JOURNAL

Purchase a bound notebook in which you will write everything relating to the project. This is your journal. It will contain your original ideas as well as ideas you get from books or from people like teachers and scientists. It will include descriptions of your experiments as well as diagrams, photographs, and written observations of all your results. Every entry should be as neat as possible and dated. Information from this journal can be used to write a report of your project, and you will want to display the journal with your completed project. A neat, orderly journal provides a complete and accurate record of your project from start to finish. It is also proof of the time you spent sleuthing out the answers to the scientific mystery you undertook to solve.

LET'S EXPLORE

This section of each chapter follows each of 20 sample experiments and provides additional questions about the problem presented in the experiment. By making small changes to some part of the sample experiment, new results are achieved. Think about why these new results might have happened.

SHOW TIME!

You can use the format of the sample experiment to design your own experiments to solve the questions asked in "Let's Explore." Your own experiment should follow the sample experiment's format and include a single question about one idea, a list of necessary materials, a detailed step-by-step procedure, written results with diagrams, graphs, and charts if they seem helpful, and a conclusion answering and explaining the question. Include any information you found through research to clarify your answer. When you design your own experiments, make sure to get adult approval if supplies or procedures other than those given in this book are used.

If you want to make a science fair project, study the information listed here and after each sample experiment in the book to develop your ideas into a real science fair exhibit. Use the suggestions that best apply to the project topic that you have chosen. Keep in mind that while your display represents all the work that you have done, it must tell the story of the project in such a way that it attracts and holds the interest of the viewer. So keep it simple. Do not try to cram all of your information into one place. To have more space on the display and still exhibit all your work, keep some of the charts, graphs, pictures, and other materials in your journal instead of on the display board itself.

The actual size and shape of displays can be different, depending on the local science fair officials, so you will have to check the rules for your science fair. Most exhibits are allowed to be 48 inches (122 cm) wide, 30 inches (76 cm) deep, and 108 inches (274 cm) high. These are maximum measurements and your display may be smaller than this. A three-sided backboard (see drawing) is usually the best way to display your work. Wooden panels can be hinged together, but you can also use sturdy cardboard pieces taped together to form a very inexpensive but presentable exhibit.

A good title of six words or less with a maximum of 50 characters should be placed at the top of the center panel. The title should capture the theme of the project but should not be the same as the problem statement. For example, if the problem under question is *Where are volcanoes most likely to be found?*, a good title of the project may be "Volcano Zones." The title and other headings should be neat and large enough to be readable at a distance of about 3 feet (1 meter). You can glue letters to the backboard (you can use precut letters that you buy or letters that you cut out of construction paper), or you can stencil the letters for all the titles. A short summary paragraph of about 100 words to explain the scientific principles involved is good and can be printed under the title. A person who has no knowledge of the topic should be able to easily understand the basic idea of the project just from reading the summary.

There are no set rules about the position of the information on the display. However, it all needs to be well organized, with the title and summary paragraph as the main point at the top of the center and the remaining material placed neatly from left to right under specific headings. Choices of headings will depend on how you wish to display the information. Separate headings for Problem, Procedure, Results, and Conclusion may be used.

The judges give points for how clearly you are able to discuss the project and explain its purpose, procedure, results, and conclusion. The display should be organized so that it explains everything, but your ability to discuss your project and answer the questions of the judges convinces them that you did the work and understand what you have done. Practice a speech in front of friends, and invite them to ask you questions. If you do not know the answer to a question, never guess or make up an answer or just say, "I do not know." Instead, you can say that you did not discover that answer during your research and then offer other information that you found of interest about the project. Be proud of the project and approach the judges with enthusiasm about your work.

CHECK IT OUT!

Read about your topic in many books and magazines. You are more likely to have a successful project if you are well informed about the topic. For the topics in this book, some tips are provided about specific places to look for information. Record in your journal all the information you find, and include for each source the author's name, the book title (or magazine name and article title), the numbers of the pages you read, the publisher's name, where it was published, and the year of publication.

1

Fiery Interior

PROBLEM

How can you make a model of the earth's interior?

Materials

2 sheets of white poster board, each
    22 × 28 inches (55 cm × 70 cm)
yardstick (meterstick)
scissors
red crayon
masking tape

Procedure

1. On one sheet of the poster board, draw a thermometer and the pie-shaped sections of the earth's interior layers, using the measurements shown in the diagram.

2. Cut out the 22-inch × 4-inch (55-cm × 10-cm) section that is above the thermometer bulb from the poster board.

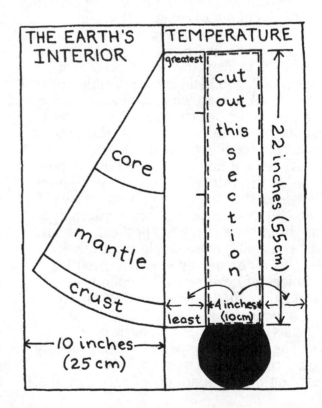

THE EARTH'S INTERIOR | TEMPERATURE

greatest

core

mantle

crust

cut out this section

least

22 inches (55cm)

4 inches (10cm)

10 inches (25 cm)

3. From the second sheet of poster board, cut two strips: one 14 inches × 28 inches (35 cm × 70 cm), and the second 8 inches × 28 inches (20 cm × 70 cm).

4. Color one whole side of the narrower strip red.

5. Cut a 10-inch (25-cm) slit 4 inches (10 cm) from the short edge of the wider strip. The slit should be centered horizontally.

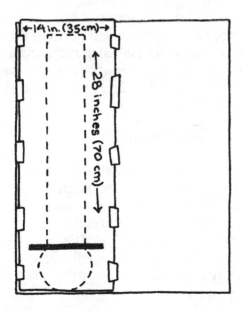

6. Tape this strip behind the cut-out section of the thermometer.

7. Insert the narrow paper strip into the slit so that the red side shows through the cut-out section of the thermometer.

8. Tape the poster to a door.

9. Slowly pull the red strip down, and observe its height at each layer of the earth's interior.

Results

Moving the red-colored strip up and down makes the temperature on the thermometer appear to increase and decrease. The temperature goes up as you near the core of the earth, and goes down as you move toward the outer layers.

Why?

The earth can be divided into three main sections: the **crust** (the outermost and coolest layer), the **mantle** (the second layer; hotter than the crust), and the **core** (the innermost and hottest layer). As the depth toward the center of the

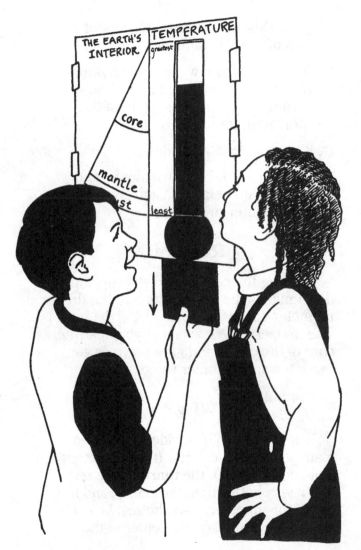

earth increases, so does the temperature. Scientists know that the earth's interior is hot because they find hot materials escaping through the surface from below. The temperature of the crust increases by about 86° Fahrenheit (30° C) for every 0.6 miles (1 km) beneath the surface. The cause of the heat is still being investigated, but three possibilities are original heat, **radioactive decay** (a breaking apart of the nucleus of an atom), and **friction** (a force that acts against motion) between great masses of rock. The original heat is the remainder of some of the heat trapped inside the earth when the earth was formed. Because radioactive decay and friction produce heat, there is an ongoing heating of the earth's interior.

LET'S EXPLORE

The layers of the earth vary in size and temperature. Use an earth science text to determine the thickness of each layer and the temperature at the top and bottom of each layer. Add this information to the model of the earth. **Science Fair Hint:** Display the model as part of your project.

SHOW TIME!

1. Scientists gain information about the earth's interior by studying its outer layer, the crust. Miners have discovered that high temperatures and great pressures prevent them from drilling at depths greater than about 5 miles (8 km). The molten rock that boils out of **volcanoes** (openings in the earth's crust from which molten rock pours) gives evidence of the makeup and temperature of the inner mantle layer. Gather these and other examples of how we know about the interior of the earth, and construct a graph with temperature on the vertical scale (bottom to top) and depth on the horizontal scale (left to right).

2. The core of the earth has two layers: the inner core and the outer core. Find out more about the core and the other layers of the earth's interior. Make a clay model of the earth, using four different-colored layers of clay to represent the different layers of the earth. Cut away a quarter section to reveal the layers. Include at least one volcano by making a small lump in the crust and showing the movement of magma from the earth's interior to the surface. Display the model along with a key to indicate which color of clay represents each layer of the earth.

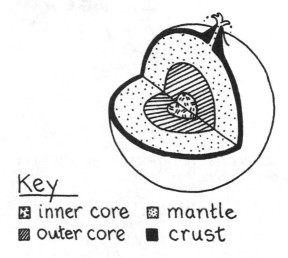

Key

⊞ inner core   ⊠ mantle
▨ outer core   ■ crust

CHECK IT OUT!

Most of the earth is not visible from the surface. Use an earth science text to discover how seismic waves are used as probes to study the unseen parts of the earth's interior. To learn more about how seismic waves are used to discover information about the earth's structure, see *Janice VanCleave's Earthquakes* (New York: Wiley, 1993), by Janice VanCleave.

2

Easy Flow

PROBLEM

How does pressure affect the rock in the asthenosphere?

Materials

measuring cup (250 ml)
tap water
9-oz (270-ml) plastic drinking glass
10 tablespoons (150 ml) cornstarch
spoon
bowl

Procedure

1. Prepare simulated "putty rock" by following these steps:

- Pour ¼ cup (63 ml) of water into the plastic glass.

- Add 1 level tablespoon (15 ml) of cornstarch and stir well. Continue adding cornstarch, 1 tablespoon (15 ml) at a time. Stir well after each addition. *NOTE: The mixture should be thick enough that it is very hard to stir.* Add a few drops of water if all of the starch will not dissolve, or add a little starch if the mixture looks thin.

2. Set the bowl on a table.

3. Hold the glass containing the putty rock in one hand, and tilt the glass slightly so that about one-half of the material flows slowly into the bowl.

4. Observe how the material flows.

5. Use the spoon to scrape the rest of the material out of the glass and into the bowl.

6. Observe how the material behaves when forced to move.

Results

The material flows easily out of the glass when not forced, but cracks and breaks if pressure is applied.

Why?

The earth can be divided into three main sections: core, mantle, and crust.

The innermost and hottest section is the core, with the mantle above it, topped by the thin outer covering called the crust. The crust and the upper portion of the mantle make up a layer that is called the **lithosphere**. Below the lithosphere is a portion of the mantle called the **asthenosphere**. In this zone, the rock making up the mantle behaves like both a liquid and a solid. Rock in the asthenosphere is thought to behave like the simulated putty rock prepared in the experiment; it flows easily if moved slowly, but thickens and breaks if pressure is applied. This ability of a solid material to flow is called **plasticity**.

LET'S EXPLORE

Would the rate at which the pressure is applied affect the results? Use the prepared simulated putty rock from the original experiment. First, apply pressure over a longer time period by placing the tip of the spoon against the surface of the putty rock. Allow the spoon to slide downward slowly. Do not push the spoon. Then, very slowly scoop out a spoonful of the material. Repeat the action, this time pushing the spoon in and lifting it back

out quickly. Notice the difference in response when more pressure is applied to the material.

SHOW TIME!

The crust of the earth is growing at areas called **mid-ocean ridges;** these ridges are divided by cracks in the crust that extend into the mantle. At the mid-ocean ridges there is decreased pressure on the **magma** (molten rock material beneath the surface of the earth). With less pressure, the magma flows more easily and moves upward through the cracks. The rising magma cools at the surface, forming a new layer on both sides of the crack. This new material pushes against the old layer of ocean floor, causing it to spread by about 1 inch (2.5 cm) each year. As the ocean widens, the continents of Europe and North America move apart.

Yet, the earth is not expanding like an inflated balloon. There are places on the crust that are sinking down into the mantle, allowing the earth's size to remain constant. You can demonstrate the rise of magma and the sinking of the crust by asking an adult to help you build two conveyor-belt models. Follow these steps for each model:

- Place one thread spool at each end of a 2-inch × 4-inch × 6-inch (5-cm × 10-cm × 15-cm) wooden board.
- Insert a nail through the hole of each spool, and hammer the tips of the nails into the board. Leave enough space between the spools and the head of the nails so that the spools turn easily.
- Connect the two spools by wrapping a strip of paper around the center of each spool and taping the strip together.
- Use a pencil to mark a starting line across each strip.

Turn the two models on their sides, end to end, with the spools facing you. Move each paper strip as needed to bring the starting lines directly above the two inner spools. Using your fingers, move the lower part of the paper strips toward the center, so that the paper strips move up and over the inner spools. This action causes the lines to move apart, representing the separation of the ocean floor as magma rises. To represent the sinking of the crust into the earth, move the paper strips in opposite directions.

board
2×4×6
inches
(5×10×15)
cm

nail

3

Riser

PROBLEM

How does density affect the movement of magma?

Materials

tap water
quart (liter) jar with lid
red food coloring
spoon
1 cup (250 ml) vegetable oil
timer

Procedure

1. Pour the water into the jar.

2. Add ten drops of the food coloring and stir.

3. Slowly add the oil.

4. Secure the lid.

5. Hold the jar so that the light from a window or desk lamp shines through the liquid in the jar.

oil

colored water

6. Slowly turn the jar until it is upside down, and then return it to its original position.

7. Observe and record the movement of the contents inside the jar for about 30 seconds.

Results

When you first pour the oil into the jar, it floats on top of the colored water. After you tip the jar, most of the oil immediately rises again to rest above the colored water, and small bubbles of oil continue to rise for a short period of time.

Why?

The separation of the two liquids is due to their being **immiscible**, meaning they do not mix. The differences in the **densities** (a comparison of the "heaviness" of materials) of the water and oil result in the denser water sinking to the bottom and the less dense oil floating to the top. Like the oil, magma, which is less dense than the rock around it, tends to rise to the surface. Magma begins its upward movement from depths of 35 miles to 50 miles (56 km to 80 km)

beneath the earth's crust. This upward journey can be caused by pressures within the earth, but more often magma rises because its density is lower than that of surrounding material.

LET'S EXPLORE

Does shaking the bottle longer affect the results? Repeat the original experiment, shaking the jar vigorously for 5 seconds. Record your observations every 5 minutes for 30 minutes, and then continue checking every hour until no further changes occur. Shaking the oil and water can be used to simulate mixing magma with denser materials. How does mixing the materials affect the material of lesser density? **Science Fair Hint:** Diagrams showing the contents of the jar at different time intervals can be made and used as part of a project display.

SHOW TIME!

1. Unless restricted by pressure, hot materials expand (get larger) and cold materials contract (get smaller). All rock materials do not expand at the same rate; thus, within the earth some of the heated rocks expand and become less dense than the surrounding rock material. You can demonstrate the difference in the densities of a compressed material and the same material when it is expanded. To do so, roll a lemon-sized piece of clay into a ball. Then, shape another similar-sized piece of clay into an open box; be sure to make the box as large as possible. Place both pieces of clay on the surface of a container of water.

2. To demonstrate the way one material will rise through another due to differences in density, fill a plastic dishwashing liquid bottle halfway with vegetable oil and secure the lid. Fill a small aquarium with water. Add a few drops of blue food coloring to the water and stir, making the water lightly colored. Turn the dishwashing liquid bottle on its side and push it down to the bottom of the aquarium. Open the spout and gently squeeze the bottle. Use photographs of the experiment as part of a project display.

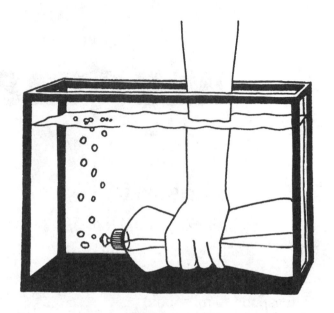

CHECK IT OUT!

At times it appears that magma moves through solid rock. By a process called **stoping**, blocks of solid rock in the path of magma are broken, melted, and added to the flowing hot, liquid rock. Find out more about magma. Does magma always reach the earth's surface? Learn about the effects that the movement of magma has on the earth's crust, such as the production of earthquakes.

4

Magma Flow

PROBLEM

How does temperature affect the movement of magma?

Materials

teaspoon (5-ml spoon)
soft margarine
small baby-food jar
cereal bowl
warm tap water
timer

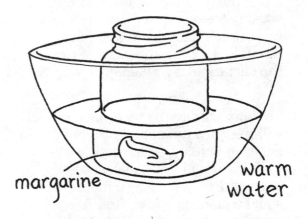

margarine   warm water

Procedure

1. Fill the teaspoon (5-ml spoon) with margarine.

2. Using your finger, push the margarine out of the spoon and into the baby-food jar so that the glob of margarine is centered in the bottom of the jar.

3. Hold the jar in your hand and turn it on its side.

4. Observe any movement of the margarine.

5. Fill the bowl halfway with warm (slightly hotter than room temperature) tap water.

6. Set the baby-food jar in the warm water.

7. After three minutes, pick up the jar and turn it on its side.

8. Again, observe any movement made by the glob of margarine.

Results

At first the margarine inside the tilted jar does not move much, but heating the margarine causes it to move more freely.

Why?

As the temperature of the margarine increased, it became thinner and moved more easily. Molecules in colder materials have less energy, are closer together, and move more slowly than warmer molecules with more energy. These warm, energized molecules move away from each other, causing solids to melt and liquids to thin. Just as the temperature of the margarine affected the way it moved across the surface of the jar, the temperature of magma affects the way it moves up the volcano's **vent** (the channel of a volcano that connects the source of magma to the volcano's opening). Hot

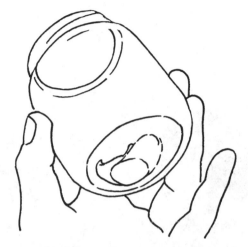

magma is thin and moves easily and quickly up the vent, while cooler magma is thick and sluggish.

LET'S EXPLORE

1. Would a different heating time affect the results? Repeat the experiment, checking the movement of the margarine every minute for six minutes. Use a thermometer to keep the temperature of the water as constant as possible, and replace the warm water each time you make an observation. Quickly replace the jar in the warm water after each testing.

water honey shampoo

2. Does the composition of the material being heated affect the results? Repeat the original experiment using other solids such as butter or chocolate candy with and without nuts.

SHOW TIME!

1. Thick liquids are said to have a high **viscosity** (the measurement of a liquid's ability to flow). Viscous liquids flow slowly, and particles dropped into the liquid fall slowly as well. Liquids such as water, honey, and shampoo can be used to simulate magma of various viscosities. Test the viscosity of each liquid by dropping a marble into a tall, slender glass filled with the liquid at room temperature. The slower the marble falls, the more viscous the liquid is.

2. Demonstrate the effect of temperature on the viscosity of the liquids by repeating the experiment above twice. First, raise the temperature of the samples by standing each glass in a jar of warm water. After three minutes, stir the liquids and use a thermometer to determine the temperature of each. Second, lower the temperature of the samples to about 50° Fahrenheit (10° C) by inserting a thermometer in each liquid sample and placing them in a refrigerator. Diagrams and the results of each experiment can be used as part of a project display.

CHECK IT OUT!

The three distinct types of magma—*andesitic*, *basaltic*, and *rhyolitic*—harden into different kinds of rock. Find out more about the characteristics of these magma types. What is their chemical composition? Where are they formed? How does the temperature of each differ? Which is the most common? For information about magma see pages 74–79 in *The Dynamic Earth*, Second Edition (New York: Wiley, 1992), by Brian J. Skinner and Stephen C. Porter.

5

Erupting Volcano

PROBLEM

How can you make a model of an erupting volcano?

Materials

16-oz (480-ml) soda bottle
large baking pan
2 measuring cups (250-ml)
1 tablespoon (15 ml) flour
1 tablespoon (15 ml) baking soda
spoon
funnel
red food coloring
1 cup (250 ml) white vinegar
tap water

Procedure

1. Place the soda bottle in the pan.
2. In one of the measuring cups, mix together the flour and baking soda.
3. Pour the flour and baking soda mixture through the funnel into the soda bottle.
4. Add 20 drops of red food coloring to the bottle.
5. Pour about one half of the vinegar into the bottle.
6. When the foaming stops, pour the remaining vinegar into the bottle.

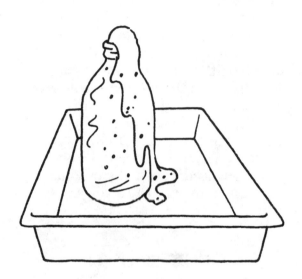

Results

Red foam bubbles out the top and then runs down the side of the bottle.

Why?

The baking soda reacts with the vinegar, producing carbon dioxide gas. As the gas forms, it expands quickly, pushing the liquid and the flour parti-cles out the top of the bottle. The mixture of the gas, flour, red food coloring, and liquid produces the foam, which simulates the foamy magma in an active volcanic eruption.

LET'S EXPLORE

1. Does the amount of vinegar affect the results? Repeat the experiment three times: first, using ¼ cup (63 ml) of vinegar and adding enough water to fill the measuring cup; second, using ½ cup (125 ml) of vinegar and filling with water; and finally, using ¾ cup (188 ml) of vinegar and filling with water. **Science Fair Hint:** Photographs can be used to represent the results.

2. Does the amount of baking soda affect the results? Repeat the original experiment twice, first using 1½ teaspoons (7.5 ml) of baking soda, and then using 2 tablespoons (30 ml) of baking soda.

3. Does the flour affect the results? Repeat the original experiment, this time omitting the flour.

SHOW TIME!

1. A volcano is a mound of rocky materials formed around a hole through which molten rock and gases are, or have been, expelled from within the earth. Build a working simulated model of a volcano by placing a soda bottle in a large pan and shaping moist soil around the bottle to form a mountain. Repeat the original experiment to simulate a volcanic eruption.

2. A more lasting model can be made by molding thin window-screen wire around the bottle, in the shape of a mountain. Mix plaster of paris by following the instructions on the box, and cover the wire with the plaster. Allow some of the plaster to flow down from the mouth of the bottle to represent the flow of **lava** (liquid rock on the surface of the earth). Allow the plaster to dry, then paint it. When the paint has dried, repeat the original experiment to simulate a volcanic eruption.

CHECK IT OUT!

Volcano cones form when lava and rock from erupting volcanoes pile up on the earth's surface. Use an earth science book to find out more about the shape of these cones. Draw diagrams and/or make cross-section clay models to represent the different volcano cones, such as the shield cone, composite cone, and cinder cone.

open soda bottle

large baking pan

mountain of soil

6

Foamy

PROBLEM

How does pressure affect the gases dissolved in magma?

Materials

cereal bowl
16-ounce (480-ml) glass soda bottle
¼ cup (63 ml) tap water
2 effervescent antacid tablets

Procedure

1. Set the bowl on a table and stand the soda bottle in it.

2. Pour the water into the bottle.

3. Break the antacid tablets in half.

4. Quickly drop the broken tablets into the bottle of water and immediately cover the mouth of the bottle with the palm of your hand.

5. Observe the contents of the bottle.

6. When it becomes difficult for you to keep your hand over the bottle because of the pressure against your palm, quickly lift your hand and observe what happens to the bottle's contents.

Results

The antacid tablets mix with the water, producing bubbles. When the bottle is covered, bubbles are seen in the water and a small amount of foam forms on the surface of the water. Uncovering the bottle produces a bubbly foam that rises within the bottle.

Why?

When the antacid tablets are combined with water, carbon dioxide gas is produced. Covering the opening of the bottle prevents the gas from escaping. As more gas is produced, the pressure inside the bottle increases. Increasing the pressure on any mixture of liquid and gas results in more gas dissolving in the liquid and a reduction in the size of the gas bubbles. Raising your hand allows the excess gas above the water to escape, which quickly reduces the pressure pushing down on the surface of the water. At this lower pressure, many gas bubbles move upward and break through the surface of the liquid. Each bubble rises, rapidly expands, and pushes some of the liquid upward, resulting in the rising foam.

A similar event happens to the dissolved gas inside magma. Deep within the earth, the pressure on magma is great and the bubbles of dissolved gas mixed with the molten rock are very small. As the magma moves upward toward the earth's surface, the pressure decreases and is the lowest at the surface. The hot liquid rock, like the liquid inside the bottle, foams as it leaves the volcano because the gas bubbles mix with the liquid and are enlarged.

LET'S EXPLORE

1. Would the size of the bottle affect the results? Repeat the experiment twice, first using a larger bottle such as a 2-liter soda bottle, and then using a smaller soda bottle.

2. Would the size of the mouth of the bottle affect the results? Repeat the experiment using bottles with larger and smaller openings.

SHOW TIME!

1. **Pumice** is a volcanic rock produced by the mixing of gases with thick magma. A piece of "mock pumice" can be produced by shaking a can of aerosol insulating foam to mix the contents. When released, the contents froths up due to expanding gas. Ask an adult to shake a can of insulating foam and then spray two mounds of foam about the size of a lemon onto a

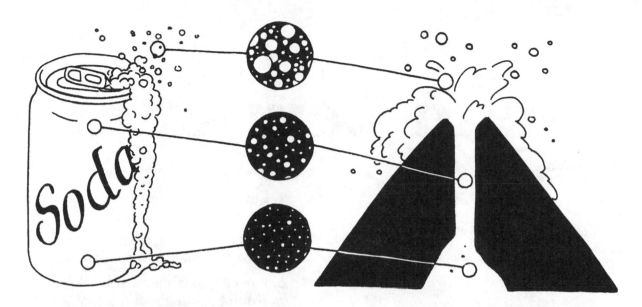

sheet of wax paper. Allow the foam to dry. Keep one piece of the dried foam intact, and ask an adult to cut the other piece in half to reveal the gas pockets inside. Display the whole and cut-in-half pieces.

2. Demonstrate the foaming action of a volcano due to pressure changes by opening a can of soda that has been shaken. This is best performed outdoors. Shake the can back and forth five or six times. Open the can, making sure the opening is pointing away from you and anyone else. Photo-

graphs taken during the experiment plus diagrams showing the relationship of the soda to magma can be displayed.

CHECK IT OUT!

Gases dissolved in magma make the liquid rock bubble and foam as the pressure changes, but what other effects do they have? Find out more about volcanic gases and how they affect the formation of volcanic rocks. What is *scoria* and how does it differ from *pumice*?

7

Spud Launcher

PROBLEM

What happens when magma hardens inside a volcano?

Materials

ruler
potato
2-liter plastic soda bottle
½ cup (125 ml) white vinegar
outdoor table
dish towel
rubber band
scissors
bathroom tissue
1 teaspoon (5 ml) baking soda

Procedure

NOTE: This is an outdoor activity.
1. Ask an adult to prepare a potato cork by following these instructions:

a. Cut a 1-inch (2.5-cm) cube from a potato.

b. Press the mouth of the soda bottle into the center of the cube.

c. Push down while twisting the bottle around to cut about halfway through the cube.

d. Carefully separate the bottle from the newly formed potato cork.

2. Pour the vinegar into the bottle.

3. Lay the towel on the table.

4. Place the bottle in an upright position in the center of the towel.

5. Fold the towel up the sides of the bottle, leaving only the mouth of the bottle exposed.

6. Secure the towel around the bottle with the rubber band.

7. Cut a 3-inch (7.5-cm) strip of bathroom tissue.

8. Spread the baking soda across the center of the tissue.

9. Roll the paper around the baking soda. Secure the packet by twisting the ends of the tissue.

baking soda   paper tissue

10. Drop the packet of baking soda into the bottle and stop the bottle with the potato cork.

11. Stand about 1 yard (1 m) away from the bottle and observe.

Results

In a short period of time, the potato cork pops out of the bottle and is propelled upward.

Why?

The paper roll opens in the liquid, and the baking soda and vinegar mix together, producing carbon dioxide gas. As the amount of this gas increases inside the bottle, pressure increases in all directions, including on the bottom of the potato cork. With enough pressure, the cork is pushed out of the bottle with enough force to propel it through the air. This experiment can be related to the eruption of a volcano that has a hardened plug of magma in the top of its vent left over from an earlier eruption. The plug of magma prevents gas from bubbling to the surface and escaping. As in the bottle, the trapped gas builds up pressure

until finally the magma plug is blown out. *NOTE: The towel covering the bottle is a safety precaution in the event that the potato plug is not pushed out and the pressure breaks the bottle.*

LET'S EXPLORE

WARNING: When exploring ways to change the original experiment, DO NOT seal the bottle with a cap or a tight-fitting cork.

Does the amount of gas affect the results? The amount of reacting materials (baking soda and vinegar) regulates the production of carbon dioxide gas. Repeat the original experiment four times. First use ½ teaspoon (2.5 ml) of baking soda, and then increase the baking soda to 2 teaspoons (10 ml). Repeat again, keeping the amount of baking soda constant but changing the amount of vinegar. First use ¼ cup (63 ml) of vinegar, and then increase the vinegar to 1 cup (250 ml).

SHOW TIME!

Discover more about volcanic eruptions. Make drawings that can be displayed and a chart showing names and locations of the different volcano types.

- Violent eruption with very thick magma and lots of gas. Magma often hardens before leaving the vent, resulting in an explosion with ash and rock fragments propelled upward.

- Active eruption with thin magma containing large amounts of gas. Hot lava shoots out the top of the volcano.

- Quiet eruption with thick magma containing small amounts of gas. Thick lava forms a huge dome.

- Quiet eruption with thin magma containing small amounts of gas. Watery lava flows out in a steady stream.

CHECK IT OUT!

Volcanoes with a magma plug have the most violent eruptions, but the other types of eruptions also cause great changes in the land and affect the lives of many people. Find out more about the effects caused by erupting volcanoes such as Krakatoa in 1883 on an Indonesian island, Mount St. Helens in 1980 in the state of Washington, and Mount Pinatubo in 1991 in the Philippines.

TYPES OF VOLCANIC ERUPTIONS			
Eruption	**Magma**	**Lava**	**Example (Name and Location)**
violent	thick; large amount of gas	none; ash and rocks	Mount St. Helens, Washington State
active			
quiet			

8

Pushing and Pulling

PROBLEM

Why are more volcanoes found in areas of great crustal movement?

Materials

sheet of typing paper
quarter
pencil with new eraser
thermometer
timer
helper

Procedure

1. Place the sheet of paper on a table, and lay the coin in the center.

2. Draw an outline around the coin. Remove the coin when you are finished.

3. Lay the thermometer next to the paper.

4. Allow the thermometer to lie undisturbed for five minutes and then read and record the temperature.

5. Press the pencil eraser against the thermometer bulb for ten seconds. *WARNING: Be careful not to press so hard that you break the bulb.*

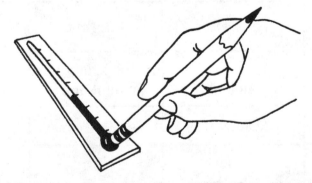

6. Read and record the temperature shown on the thermometer. Do not touch the bulb with your fingers.

7. Ask your helper to start the timer as you rub the eraser back and forth against the paper inside the circle. Rub as quickly and as hard as possible without tearing the paper.

8. Stop rubbing when your helper notifies you that ten seconds have passed.

9. Immediately, gently press the eraser against the bulb of the thermometer (as before, take care not to press so hard that you break the thermometer).

10. Observe the thermometer.

11. When the temperature reading stops changing, read and record the temperature.

Results

The temperature reading increased when the bulb of the thermometer was touched by the eraser after the eraser had been rubbed against the paper.

Why?

Moving one surface against another, such as the eraser against the paper, causes friction. Friction is a force that acts against motion, and this resistance to motion produces heat. The increase in the temperature of the eraser was a result of the friction produced by the pushing and pulling motion of the pencil eraser against the paper.

According to the **plate tectonic theory**, the crust of the earth is broken into large plates that float on a hot fluid. Volcanoes and earthquakes occur along boundaries where plates collide. It is now understood that large amounts of heat can be produced when one great, massive crustal plate moves against another crustal plate. This crustal movement causes friction, friction produces heat, and the heat vaporizes liquids and melts rocks. The pressure of these heated materials breaks the earth's crust, spraying the hot steamy materials into the air, and creating a volcanic eruption.

LET'S EXPLORE

Do the types of surfaces rubbed together affect the amount of heat produced? Repeat the experiment, rubbing the eraser against different surfaces such as cardboard, a carpet, various cloth samples, and a wooden block. Be sure to use the same force and time for each material. *NOTE: Since the eraser can remove color from surfaces, use small samples of materials that nobody wants.* **Science Fair Hint:** The surface samples can be displayed, along with a small diagram of a thermometer noting the resulting temperatures.

SHOW TIME!

1. Rice grains can be used to demonstrate that friction between rocks causes heat. Fill a quart (liter) jar with

jar, and shake it vigorously for 30 seconds. Immediately unscrew the cap, replace the thermometer, and measure the temperature of the rice.

2. Read about earthquakes and volcanoes. Make a list of the locations and names of volcanoes and areas with frequent earthquakes. On a globe or large world map, place labels with the letter E for earthquake areas and a V for the volcano locations. Compare the locations of earthquakes and volcanoes around the world to determine if there are more volcanoes in areas with greater crustal movement.

CHECK IT OUT!

Volcanoes are located in two main regions on earth, called *belts*. One belt, called the Ring of Fire, circles the Pacific Ocean. The other belt is located along the shores of the Caribbean and Mediterranean seas. These belts outline where great crustal movement occurs. Find out more about the movement of the earth's crust by reading about the plate tectonics theory in earth science books.

1 cup (250 ml) of uncooked rice. Insert a thermometer. After one minute, read and record the temperature. Remove the thermometer, secure the lid on the

9

Volcano Types

PROBLEM

How are composite volcanoes formed?

Materials

4 or 5 ice cubes
2 wide-mouthed, clear-glass,
    quart (liter) jars
cold tap water
small baby-food jar
warm tap water
red food coloring
spoon
modeling clay
pencil
scissors
ruler
drinking straw

Procedure

1. Place the ice cubes in one of the quart (liter) jars. Fill the jar with cold tap water.

2. Fill the baby-food jar to overflowing with warm tap water.

3. Add five drops of food coloring to the baby-food jar and stir.

4. Cover the mouth of the baby-food jar with a ball of clay.

5. Use a pencil to punch two holes through the clay stopper.

6. Cut a 4-inch (10-cm) piece from the drinking straw and insert it into one of the holes made in the clay stopper. The top of the straw should extend slightly above the clay.

7. Push the clay around the straw to seal the opening.

8. Place the baby-food jar inside the empty quart (liter) jar.

9. Remove any unmelted ice cubes from the first large jar, and pour the chilled water into the second jar (the one containing the baby-food jar). Completely fill the second jar with the chilled water.

10. Observe the contents of the second large jar for two or three minutes.

Results

The warm, colored water rises upward until it reaches the surface of the cool water. After a while, the layer of colored water at the surface starts to fall.

Why?

Water molecules, like all matter, are spaced closer together when cold and move farther apart when heated. The density, which is a scientific way of measuring "heaviness," is less for the warm, colored water than the colder, clear water because of this spacing. The less dense warm water is more **buoyant** (able to float) than is the denser chilled water; thus, the warm, colored water rises to the top and forms a layer at the surface

cold water

warm water

above the chilled water. As the warm water cools, its molecules move closer together, the water becomes denser, and it begins to sink.

The slow movement of the warm water can be compared to the movement of hot magma during what is called a *quiet eruption* (see Experiment 7 for the different types of volcanic eruptions). The hotter the magma, the farther apart are its molecules and thus the less dense it is. The hot, buoyant magma rises from the **magma chamber** (pool of magma deep within the earth) to the surface through a central opening known as a vent (the channel of a volcano that connects the source of magma to the volcano's opening). In your model, the straw represents the vent. Like the warm water in the straw, hot magma rises through the vent to the surface. The colored water began its fall as it cooled, but during most quiet volcanic eruptions the magma first fills a **crater** (the bowl-shaped depression at the top of a volcano) before flowing out as lava (magma that has reached the surface). The lava eventually cools, forming a hard layer at the top and down the sides of the volcano; thus, the volcano grows larger with each eruption.

Composite volcanoes are cone-shaped volcanoes formed by alternate layers of solidified lava and rocks. Each layer is made by a different type of volcanic activity. The lava layer is formed as previously described during quiet eruptions, but the rock layers are the result of violent eruptions that expel rock fragments.

LET'S EXPLORE

1. Would more openings in the clay affect the results? Repeat the experiment, adding a third hole and a straw. Besides the main vent, some volcanoes may have smaller vents called *side vents*. **Science Fair Hint:** Photographs of the original experiment with its single vent, along with photographs of the multivent volcano, can be displayed.

2. Does the temperature of the water inside and outside the jar affect the results? Prepare a data chart as shown on the next page. Repeat the original experiment three times using the combinations in the data chart. The combination from the original experiment has been added as an example.

BABY-FOOD JAR		
Colored Water Inside	Clear Water Outside	Results
warm	cold	Colored water rises to the surface.
cold	cold	
cold	warm	
warm	warm	

SHOW TIME!

A cross section of a composite volcano often shows alternating layers of solidified lava and rock particles. This is the result of quiet eruptions in which lava was produced followed by a violent eruption that blew out ash and rock fragments. Use different colors of modeling clay to construct a cross-section model of a composite volcano. Press small rocks into the layer representing the rock fragment layer. This model can be used as part of a project display.

CHECK IT OUT!

Some of the tallest volcanoes are composite volcanoes, but there are other types, such as *cinder cone, shield,* and *volcanic dome.* Find out more about the four types of volcanoes. Which type is called a *stratovolcano?* Mount Rainier, in the state of Washington, is an example of a composite volcano. Discover the names and locations of other volcanoes representing each type.

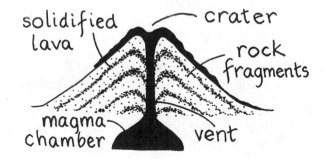

10

Too Hot!

PROBLEM

How can the strength of a magnetic field be measured and used to predict a volcanic eruption?

Materials

small iron nail
bar magnet
scissors
ruler
sewing thread
2-inch × 10-inch (5-cm × 25-cm)
   piece of cardboard
paper hole-punch

Procedure

1. Magnetize the nail by laying it on the magnet for two to three minutes.

2. Cut a 12-inch (30-cm) piece of thread, and tie one end to the center of the magnetized nail.

3. Hold the other end of the thread with one hand. Move the nail back and forth through the knot in the thread until it hangs in a horizontal position (parallel, or level, with the tabletop).

4. Bend 2 inches (5 cm) of one end of the cardboard at a right angle.

5. Use the hole-punch to make a hole in the center of the bent section of the cardboard.

6. Insert the thread up through the hole.

7. Hold the cardboard in a vertical position, and pull down on the thread until the nail rises to the top.

8. Hold the north end of the magnet next to the base of the cardboard.

9. Slowly lower the nail until one end begins to dip toward the magnet.

10. Measure the height from the pivot point on the nail to the magnet.

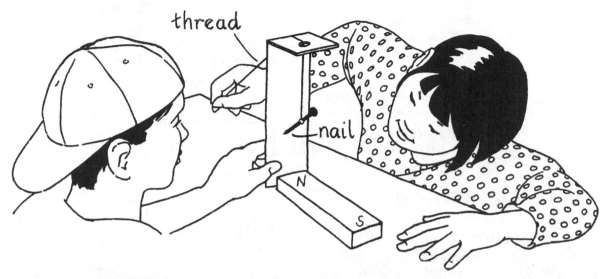

thread

nail

N

S

Results

The nail is horizontal when held at a distance above the magnet, but as the nail is moved, one end eventually dips toward the magnet. The distance between the pivot point and the magnet will vary depending on the strength of the magnet.

Why?

A **magnetometer** is an instrument used to measure the magnetic strength of a material. The magnetometer in this experiment is not very accurate, but it does indicate the strength of the magnet.

The greater the distance between the magnet and the pivot point of the magnetometer, the greater the magnetic strength.

Volcanologists (scientists who study volcanoes) have observed that when magnetic rocks are heated above 1,110° Fahrenheit (600° C), they lose their magnetism. Periodic checks with a magnetometer detect changes in the magnetic strength of the rocks in the volcano. A decrease in the magnetic strength indicates that the temperature inside is increasing. This could mean that the magma is moving and an eruption may take place soon.

LET'S EXPLORE

Would laying the other end of the magnet toward the magnetometer affect the results? Repeat the experiment, turning the magnet so that its other end faces the base of the cardboard.

SHOW TIME!

An **optical pyrometer** is an instrument used to measure the temperature of hot materials, such as hot lava flowing from a volcano. Because it is too dangerous to get near the fiery molten rock, volcanologists view the glowing material through a pyrometer, which has a wire inside its viewing chamber. The temperature of the wire is controlled by increasing or decreasing the electric current that passes through it. As the wire heats up, its color changes from red to white. The color of the lava as seen through the viewing chamber is compared to that of the wire. When the colors are the same, the temperature of the wire is assumed to be the temperature of the lava.

You can construct a model of a pyrometer. Cut a 36-inch (1-m) strip of paper adding-machine tape. Fold the strip into three equal sections; then fold it in half again to form six equal sections.

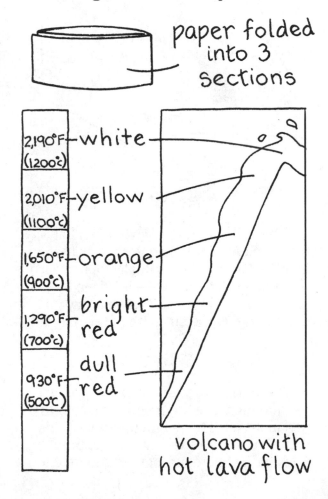

paper folded into 3 sections

2,190°F (1200°C) — white
2,010°F (1100°C) — yellow
1,650°F (900°C) — orange
1,290°F (700°C) — bright red
930°F (500°C) — dull red

volcano with hot lava flow

Unfold the strip and draw a line across each crease. Label the lines and color the sections on the strip as indicated in the diagram. On a poster board, draw a volcano and color the lava using the same colors as on the paper strip. Remember that the hotter colors will be near the mouth of the volcano. Tape this volcano poster to a wall at eye level.

In each end of a shoe box (see diagram), cut a 2-inch × 2-inch (5-cm × 5-cm) square. The squares should both be to one side of the end of the box and should be positioned directly across from each other. At one end of the box top, cut a slit large enough for the paper strip to slide though easily. The slit should be on the opposite side of the box from the cut-out squares so that when you look through one square the other is not obstructed. Cut another slit for the paper to move through in the bottom of the box directly below the slit in the box top. In the box top, about 1 inch (2.5 cm) from the slit, cut out a 2-inch × 4-inch (5-cm × 10-cm) section. Insert the strip of paper through the slits, with the labeled side facing the center of the box, and tape a pencil to each end.

Point the end of the box with the paper slit toward the poster drawing of the volcano. To determine the temperature of different parts of the lava, look through the viewing hole toward the lava as you move the paper strip until the color on the strip matches the color of the lava. Display the volcano drawing and the pyrometer.

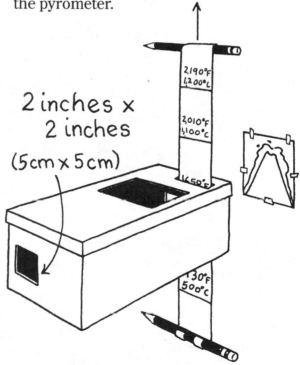

2 inches × 2 inches
(5cm × 5cm)

2,190°F
1,200°C

2,010°F
1,100°C

1,650°F

1,130°F
500°C

11

Gas Sniffers

PROBLEM

How can you test for the presence of carbon dioxide and use it to predict a volcanic eruption?

Materials

l-quart (1-liter) jar with lid
distilled water
1 teaspoon (5 ml) calcium oxide (lime used to make pickles)
spoon
baby-food jar
measuring cup
white vinegar
glass soda bottle
modeling clay
flexible drinking straw
scissors
ruler
bathroom tissue
1 teaspoon (5 ml) baking soda

Procedure

1. Prepare the carbon dioxide-testing solution called limewater, using the following steps:

   • Fill the 1-quart (1-liter) jar with distilled water.

   • Add the calcium oxide and stir.

   • Secure the lid and allow the solution to stand overnight.

2. Fill the baby-food jar three-fourths full with limewater. *NOTE: When pouring liquid out of the jar, be careful not to pour out any of the lime that has settled on the bottom of the jar, and always secure the lid on the jar.*

3. Pour ¼ cup (63 ml) of water and ¼ cup (63 ml) vinegar into the soda bottle.

clay

limewater

vinegar & water

Baking Soda

4. Press a walnut-sized piece of clay about an inch from the end of the straw closest to the flexible section.

5. Cut a 3-inch (7.5-cm) length of bathroom tissue.

6. Spread the baking soda across the center of the tissue.

7. Roll the tissue around the baking soda. Secure the packet by twisting the ends of the paper.

8. Drop the packet of baking soda into the soda bottle.

9. Immediately plug the bottle's mouth with the clay around the straw. *CAUTION: The short end of the straw should be inside the bottle. DO NOT close the opening in the straw.*

10. Hold the baby-food jar of limewater near the bottle so that the long end of the straw is beneath the surface of the limewater.

11. When the bubbling ceases, observe the limewater.

Results

As bubbles from the straw enter the clear limewater, the limewater turns milky.

Why?

Baking soda consists of the chemical compound sodium bicarbonate. When this carbonate compound reacts with vinegar (acetic acid), carbon dioxide gas is produced. Limewater is used to test for the presence of carbon dioxide gas because it reacts with carbon dioxide to form a white **insoluble** (does not dissolve) compound called calcium carbonate. This simple experiment demonstrates that the presence of a gas can be identified. Volcanologists collect gas samples from the gases escaping from **fumaroles** (volcanic vents from which only gas escapes) in order to identify and determine the quantity of each gas present. Studies of the gas content of volcanoes have revealed that the amount of water vapor, carbon dioxide, and sulfur dioxide often increases before an eruption. An increase in these gases is not enough evidence to predict an eruption, but gas studies along with other changes provide the scientists with indicators used to predict a possible volcanic eruption.

LET'S EXPLORE

1. Do other carbonated substances produce carbon dioxide when combined with acid? Repeat the original experiment, replacing the baking soda with materials that contain calcium carbonate (limestone), such as eggshells, marble chips, or white chalk.

2. Would using a different acid alter the

results? Repeat the original experiment, replacing the vinegar and water mixture with ½ cup (125 ml) of citric acid such as lemon juice or grapefruit juice.

SHOW TIME!

The massive amounts of gases (mostly water vapor) emitted from volcanoes contain thick clouds of steam, poisonous gases, and ash. This thick, choking mass can rush down the mountain at more than 100 miles (160 km) per hour, killing people and wildlife.

Carbon dioxide flows down a mountain because it is heavier than air. This can be demonstrated by pouring 1 inch (2.5 cm) of limewater into the bottom of a quart (liter) jar. Partly cover the mouth of the jar with a lid. In a small-mouthed gallon (4-liter) jug, mix together 1 teaspoon (5 ml) of baking soda, ¼ cup (63 ml) of water, and ½ cup (125 ml) of vinegar. When the fizzing stops, hold the mouth of the gallon jug over the mouth of the jar and slowly tilt the jug. Do not allow the liquid from the jug to enter the jar of limewater. Secure the lid on the jar, and observe the limewater after 24 hours; a thin layer of white powder will be on the bottom of the jar. The invisible, heavier-than-air carbon dioxide flows into the jar, and reacts with the limewater to produce the insoluble calcium carbonate seen on the jar's bottom. Display diagrams of the sequence of events in this reaction. Ask a chemistry teacher to assist you in writing the chemical equations for the reactions.

CHECK IT OUT!

1. Collecting gases from an eruption is not a job for the faint at heart. Find out how these brave scientists secure gas samples. What type of protective clothing must be worn by the collectors? What instruments are used in the collecting process?

2. Volcanoes produce massive amounts of gases such as carbon monoxide, carbon dioxide, hydrogen sulfide, chlorine, hydrogen chloride, sulfur dioxide, and water vapor, as well as other gases, all of which are released into the atmosphere. Find out more about the effect of these gases on the environment.

12

Tilt

PROBLEM

How does a tiltmeter give clues to where a volcano is likely to occur?

Materials

pencil
2 5-oz (150-ml) paper cups
drinking straw
modeling clay
shallow baking pan
tap water

Procedure

1. Use the point of the pencil to make a hole through the side of one paper cup near the bottom edge. The hole must be small enough so that the straw will fit tightly in it.

paper cup

pencil

2. Remove the pencil and insert about ½ inch (1.3 cm) of one end of the straw into the hole.

3. Use a small piece of clay to form a seal around the hole.

4. Poke a hole near the bottom edge of the second cup.

5. Place the other end of the straw in the hole.

6. Seal the opening with a piece of clay.

7. Place the connected cups in the center of the pan.

8. Fill both cups halfway with water.

9. Lift one end of the pan so that it is about 2 inches (5 cm) above the table.

10. Observe the contents of each cup.

Results

The water in each of the two cups is at the same height before the pan is raised. Raising the pan causes the amount of water to decrease in the elevated cup and to increase in the lower cup.

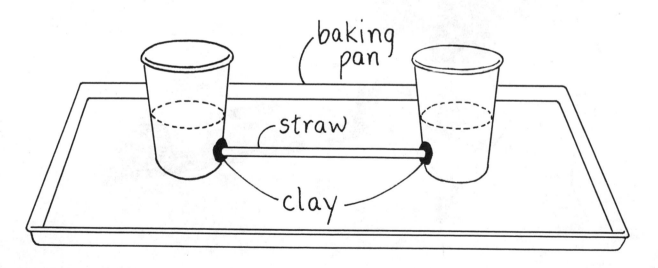

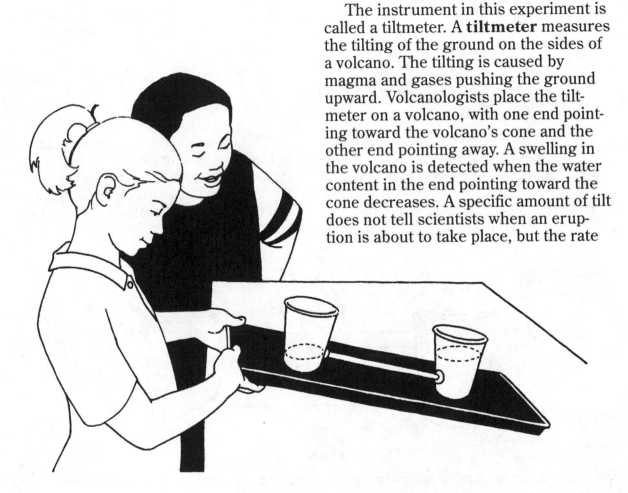

Why?

The instrument in this experiment is called a tiltmeter. A **tiltmeter** measures the tilting of the ground on the sides of a volcano. The tilting is caused by magma and gases pushing the ground upward. Volcanologists place the tiltmeter on a volcano, with one end pointing toward the volcano's cone and the other end pointing away. A swelling in the volcano is detected when the water content in the end pointing toward the cone decreases. A specific amount of tilt does not tell scientists when an eruption is about to take place, but the rate at which the volcano swells provides clues. An unusually large swelling in a short period of time tells them that an eruption is most likely on the way.

LET'S EXPLORE

1. Does the length of the straw affect the results? Repeat the experiment two times, first using a straw cut in half, and then using two straws connected by pushing the end of one straw into the end of the second straw.

2. Do the sizes of the cups affect the results? Repeat the original experiment twice, first using smaller cups, and then using larger cups.

SHOW TIME!

A carpenter's level is like a tiltmeter. When the bubble in the liquid-filled glass cylinder is in the middle, the carpenter's level is exactly level or horizontal. Use a carpenter's level as a tiltmeter to demonstrate the tilt of the earth as magma and gases cause the earth's crust to expand. Cut a 2-inch (5-cm) hole in the bottom end of a large shoe box. Place a deflated balloon inside the box with its mouth pulled through the hole. Fill the box with soil, making the surface as level as possible. Place the carpenter's level on top of the soil. Ask a helper to blow up the balloon as you watch the movement of the bubble in the level. Photographs and diagrams of the position of the bubble can be used as part of a project display.

CHECK IT OUT!

Some volcano tiltmeters are so sensitive that they can detect the slightest movement in the earth's crust produced by the pull from the moon's gravity. Find out more about tiltmeters. How do the different types vary?

13

Stretch

PROBLEM

How does an extensiometer measure the change in size of a volcano?

Materials

2 sheets of construction paper
modeling clay
5-inch (12.5-cm) long pencil
12-inch (30-cm) piece of 14-gauge,
   single-strand wire
empty thread spool
scissors
ruler
string
masking tape
paper clip

Procedure

1. Place the 2 sheets of paper on a table with the ends overlapping each other about 6 inches (15 cm).

2. Place one walnut-sized lump of clay on each piece of paper.

3. Press the pencil, eraser side up, into one of the clay mounds.

4. Run the wire through the hole in the thread spool.

5. Bend the ends of the wire as shown in the diagram, and stick the ends of the wire into the second mound of clay.

6. Cut a 16-inch (40-cm) piece of string.

7. Tie one end of the string around the top of the pencil and secure it with a piece of tape.

8. Pull the string across the empty spool.

9. Attach the paper clip to the end of the string.

10. Observe the height of the paper clip above the surface of the paper.

11. Separate the pencil and the thread spool by slowly moving the papers outward about 1 inch (2.5 cm).

12. Again, observe the height of the paper clip above the paper.

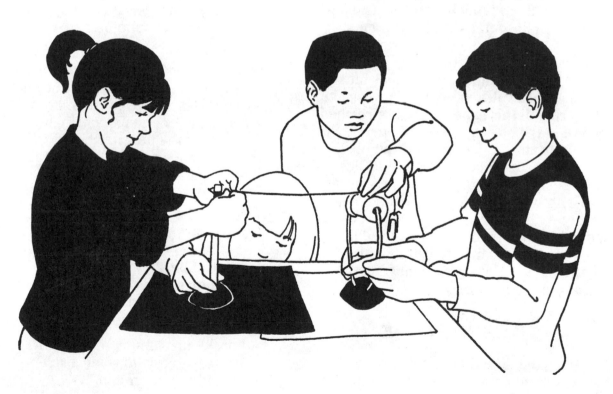

Results

The height of the paper clip above the paper increases as the distance between the pencil and thread spool increases.

Why?

The instrument constructed in this experiment is a model of an extensiometer. **Extensiometers** are instruments used by volcanologists to measure changes in the diameter of a volcano. Scientists firmly anchor two poles into the floor of a volcano's crater. A wire, like the string in this experiment, is stretched between the poles and secured to one. A weight is attached to the free end of the wire. If the distance between the poles changes, due to a swelling of the volcano, the length of the wire between the poles changes. The amount of movement of one or both poles can be measured by the length of the material stretched between the poles or the change in the height of the hanging weight.

LET'S EXPLORE

1. Does the direction of the motion affect the results? Repeat the experiment, moving the paper at angles to each other. **Science Fair Hint:** Photographs of the extensiometer, showing the position of the paper and the height of the paper clip, can be displayed. All photographs should include: a background as a reference point, an object of known size for comparison, and a ruler. Be sure to number sequences of photos.

2. Does the material between the poles have to be flexible? Repeat the original experiment, replacing the string with an 18-inch (45-cm) dowel rod that has a diameter equal to or smaller than that of the pencil. Observe the change in the amount the rod that extends past the spool as the papers are moved.

SHOW TIME!

1. Scales can be added to the simple extensiometer so that the differences in the distances can be measured and recorded.

   a. For the instrument made with string, use clay to stand a ruler behind the paper clip.

b. For the extensiometer made with a dowel rod, make a measuring tape by placing a strip of masking tape along the edge of a metric ruler. Use a pen to copy the ruler increments onto 6 inches (15 cm) of the tape. Remove the tape from the ruler and attach it to the end of the rod that extends over the spool.

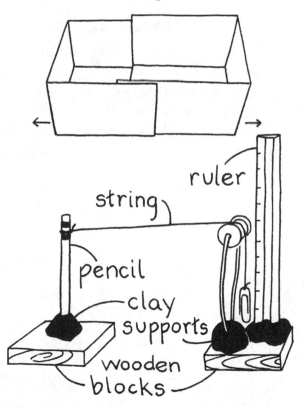

2. Here is another way to make an extensiometer model. Cut a shoe box in half. Put the two pieces of the box back together so that the edges overlap by about 4 inches (10 cm). Fill the box with dirt. Make the extensiometer as in the original experiment, but place the end posts of the extensiometer on wooden blocks instead of paper. Place the blocks on the surface of the soil, one at each end of the box. Include a measuring stick supported by a glob of clay next to the hanging paper clip. Read the height of the bottom of the paper clip, and then ask a helper to move the ends of the box outward a short distance. Determine the distance that the box was moved.

CHECK IT OUT!

An easier way of measuring the surface-distance changes is to use a long steel tape measure. Find out more about the inflation or contraction of volcanoes and ways of measuring these changes. How accurate is the use of the steel measuring tape? How would heat affect the steel? How can photographs be used to measure a volcano's change in size?

14

Taking a Volcano's Pulse

PROBLEM

How does a seismometer record the shaking caused by earthquakes and movements of magma below the earth's surface?

Materials

cardboard box, measuring about 12
  inches (30 cm) on each side
scissors
ruler
string
pencil
5-oz (150-ml) paper cup
masking tape
small mirror about 4 inches (10 cm)
  square
rice
2 books
flashlight
adult helper

Procedure

1. Turn the box on its side with the opening facing outward.

2. Ask an adult helper to cut a circle measuring 2 inches (5 cm) in diameter in the center of the top of the box.

3. Cut a 24-inch (60-cm) piece of string.

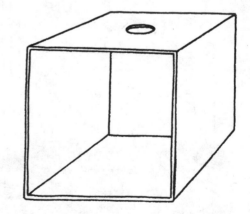

4. Use the point of the pencil to punch a hole on each side of the cup just below the rim.

5. Tie the free ends of the string in the holes in the cup, so the string forms a handle for the cup.

6. Tape the mirror to the side of the cup.

7. Fill the cup with rice.

8. Push the center of the string through the hole in the top of the box so that the cup hangs with the mirror facing you.

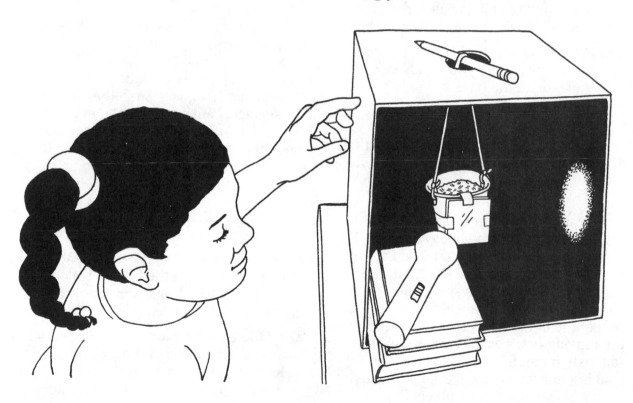

9. Place the pencil through the loop formed by the string and across the hole in the top of the box.

10. Place the books inside the box.

11. Lay the flashlight on top of the books, and position it so that the light hits the mirror and then reflects onto the right side of the box.

12. Watch the spot of light on the wall of the box while you gently tap the left side of the box.

Results

The light spot moves back and forth, in a zigzag pattern, on the wall of the box.

Why?

Because of **inertia** (resistance to a change in motion), the heavy cup resists moving as the box is shaken and tries to remain where it is. As a result, the cup lags behind and begins swinging. The swinging of the cup causes the mirror to reflect the light in different directions on the moving box's wall. A **seismometer** (an instrument used to measure the shaking energy of an earthquake) uses a very heavy suspended object that responds to movement in the same way. Instead of a light source, a recording pen is attached to the suspended object; if the ground beneath the seismometer moves, the weight resists the movement, but the pen touches and records the vibrations on paper. This printed record is called a **seismogram**.

Prior to a volcanic eruption, there may be many strong earthquakes per hour or hundreds of small earthquakes. These quakes are produced as the moving magma and hot gases push their way to the surface, causing the earth to expand and crack. Volcanologists can use seismometers to feel the pulse of the earth, aiding in the prediction of impending volcanic eruptions.

LET'S EXPLORE

1. Does the weight of the cup affect the degree to which the light is reflected? Fill the cup with heavier materials such as rocks or lead fishing weights.

2. Would the direction of the earthquake affect the pattern of the light formed? Repeat the experiment, tapping the box on the top, back, and right sides.

SHOW TIME!

Another seismometer that uses a light beam can be constructed by placing a bowl full of water on top of a box. Ask a helper to hold a flashlight so that its beam of light falls on the surface of the

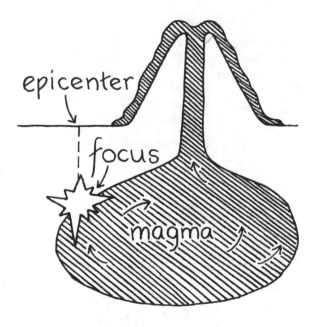

water and is reflected to a nearby paper screen. Watch the spot of light on the screen while you tap the side of the box with your hand.

As part of a project display, attach a diagram of a cutaway view of a volcano to the side of the box. The diagram should show the moving magma, the **focus** (the underground point of origin of an earthquake), and the **epicenter** (the point on the earth's surface directly above the focus of an earthquake). Tape the paper screen to one wall of your display, and demonstrate the light-beam seismometer.

CHECK IT OUT!

The exact location of an earthquake's focus is very important to volcanologists when determining where a volcano might erupt. Find out more about determining the focus location of earthquakes. How are the seismometers used? How does spacing apart the seismometers aid in pinpointing these locations?

![volcano icon] **15**

Lifter

PROBLEM

How does intrusive volcanism (movement beneath the earth's surface) change the shape of the earth's crust?

Material

knife (to be used only by an adult)
clear plastic drinking glass
scissors
large tube of toothpaste (remove the cap)
½ cup (125 ml) of soil
adult helper

Procedure

Ask an adult to use a knife to cut a hole in the bottom of the glass from the inside, then use scissors to make the hole as large as the mouth of the toothpaste tube.

2. Hold your finger over the hole in the bottom while you pour the soil into the glass.

3. Insert the mouth of the toothpaste tube into the hole.

4. Ask your helper to hold the glass while you press against the tube to force the toothpaste into the glass.

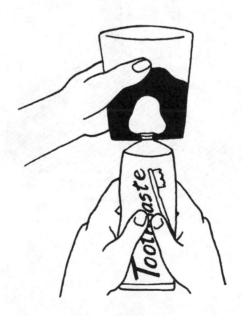

5. Observe the contents of the glass as the toothpaste enters. Pay special attention to the surface of the soil.

Results

As the toothpaste rises in the glass, the soil is pushed upward, forming a dome-shaped rise in the soil's surface.

Why?

Liquid rock beneath the earth's surface is called magma. Pressure on pools of magma deep within the earth forces the molten rock toward the surface. This movement of magma within the earth is referred to as **intrusive volcanism**. Intrusive volcanism is responsible for different types of **intrusions** (flows of magma that cool and harden before they reach the surface). Intrusions have many shapes because magma hardens in many positions as it cools. The hardened or solidified magma forms **igneous rock**. A dome-like intrusion is called a **laccolith**. A laccolith is formed when magma pushes overlying rock upward. The toothpaste simulates the formation of a laccolith. The mushroom-shaped paste pushes the overlying contents of the glass upward, producing a mound on the soil's surface.

soil
rocks
toothpaste

second plastic glass inside the glass of soil. Ask your helper to push down on this glass to restrict the movement of soil as you force toothpaste into the glass. **Science Fair Hint:** Use the description in SHOW TIME! to identify the type of intrusion formed. Label and display the glass from this and the original experiment.

LET'S EXPLORE

What would happen if rock layers restricted the upward movement of the magma? Repeat the experiment, adding rocks to the soil mixture and standing a

SHOW TIME!

1. Bodies of intrusive igneous rock are classified according to their shape and relationship to surrounding rock. Use the description of each type of rock structure and the diagram to build a

clay model showing the rock structures formed by intrusive activities. This model can be used as part of a project display.

- **Batholiths**—large intrusions below the earth's surface.

- **Dikes**—narrow, vertical intrusions that rise and break through horizontal rock layers.

- **Laccoliths**—mushroom- or dome-shaped intrusions that push up the overlaying rock layer.

- **Sills**—thin, horizontal intrusions sandwiched between other rock layers.

- **Stocks**—intrusions below the earth's surface; smaller than batholith bodies.

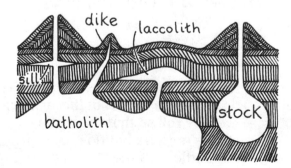

2. Granite is the most common type of intrusive igneous rock. The composition of granite can vary depending on the kinds and proportions of minerals present in the magma that formed it. Different samples of granite can be purchased at a rock shop, or collect your own samples. Use these as part of a display showing the different shapes of intrusions and their composition.

CHECK IT OUT!

Domed mountains, such as the Henry Mountains of southern Utah or the Black Hills of South Dakota, are broad, circular mountains formed when layers of rock are lifted. Find out more about the surface landforms created by intrusions. What is the surface like in areas where the different intrusions are exposed when rocks around them are worn away by erosion? Examples of exposed batholiths are the Sierra Nevada mountains of California. Identify other exposed intrusion areas.

16

Slow Mover

PROBLEM

How does the viscosity of lava affect its flow rate?

Materials

scissors
clear plastic dish-detergent bottle with
    pull top
ruler
marking pen
modeling clay
jar with a mouth slightly smaller than
    the base of the dish-detergent bottle
pitcher
cold tap water
timer
adult helper

Procedure

1. Prepare a **viscometer** (meter used to measure the flow rate of a fluid) by following these steps:

a. Ask your adult helper to cut off the bottom of the detergent bottle.

b. Hold the bottle upside down. The bottom edge of the detergent bottle will now be referred to as the top. Draw two straight, horizontal lines on the bottle: one about 1 inch (2.5 cm) below the open top, and the other 4 inches (10 cm) below the first line.

c. Label the top line START and the bottom line STOP.

d. Make sure the pull top of the bottle is closed.

e. Place a role of clay around the mouth of the jar.

f. Rest the detergent bottle upside down on the mouth of the jar. Mold the clay roll so that the bottle stands upright, but do not secure the bottle with the clay.

2. Fill the pitcher with cold tap water.

3. Pour the water into the open end of the detergent bottle until the water is about ½ inch (1.3 cm) above the START line.

4. Lift the bottle and pull the top open.

5. Immediately return the bottle to the mouth of the jar and start the timer when the water level reaches the START line.

6. Stop the timer when the water level reaches the STOP line.

VISCOMETER

7. Repeat the procedure three times.

8. Average the flow time of cold tap water by adding the three flow-time results together and dividing the sum by three. The following example shows the author's flow-time results and the calculated average flow time.

Sum of flow-time results (seconds)
= 39.2 + 39.4 + 39.3
= 117.9 seconds

Average flow time = 117.9 seconds ÷ 3
= 39.3 seconds

Results

The flow time will vary with the shape of the bottle used. The author's average flow time for cold water from the faucet was 39.3 seconds.

Why?

The amount of time it takes a liquid to flow out of a container depends on its viscosity. The viscosity of a liquid is the resistance of the liquid to flowing; or its stickiness. Water has a low viscosity and flows quickly out of the open viscometer.

Different types of lava have different viscosities. Some are so thick and sticky and have such a high viscosity that they creep along, moving only a few yards (m) per day. Others have a low viscosity, and flow a few miles (km) per hour.

LET'S EXPLORE

1. How does the viscosity of other liquids compare to the viscosity of water? Repeat the experiment using liquids such as oil, dishwashing liquid, honey, and/or syrup. Wipe out the viscometer after each test with a paper towel or prepare separate instruments for each liquid tested. Compare the flow times of each liquid.

2. Does the temperature of the liquid affect its viscosity? Repeat this experiment twice: first by reducing the temperature of the liquids by chilling them in the freezer, and then by heating the liquids by placing a cup of each in a bowl of warm tap water. **Science Fair Hint:** Prepare bar graphs to display the results of each testing liquid. Label the results from the room-temperature testing as medium temperature.

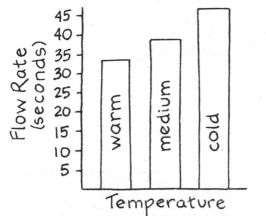

VISCOSITY AND TEMPERATURE

Flow Rate (seconds) vs. Temperature bar graph showing warm (~33), medium (~39), cold (~46)

of the second volcano. Again, observe the flow rate of the liquid as it flows down the volcano's sides. Take photographs of the experiments and use them as part of a project display.

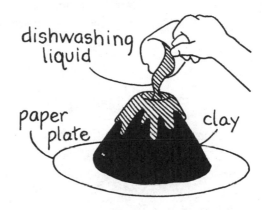

dishwashing liquid
paper plate
clay

SHOW TIME!

What happens to the flow rate of lava when it contains particles of a solid? Build two volcanoes out of clay. Make each volcano about 6 inches (15 cm) tall with a small bowl-shaped indention at the top, and put each in the center of a plate. Pour 1 cup (250 ml) of dishwashing liquid into the indention on the top of one volcano. Observe the flow rate of the liquid as it overflows and runs down the side of the clay mountain. Mix ¾ cup (188 ml) dishwashing liquid with ¼ cup (63 ml) of sand. Pour this mixture in the top

CHECK IT OUT!

Hot, thin lava flows freely and forms smooth layers when cooled. Cool, thick lava breaks and tumbles forward rather than flowing. It produces a rough texture when cooled. Find out more about the movement of lava and its appearance when cooled. Describe *pahoehoe* and *aa*, Hawaiian names for two different types of lava. (See Experiment 17 for more on this subject.)

17

Fire Rocks

PROBLEM

What type of rock is formed when lava cools?

Materials

small box with a lid
marbles

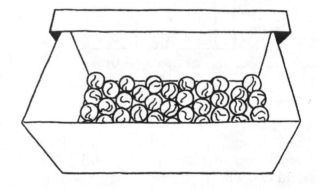

Procedure

1. Cover the bottom of the box with a single layer of marbles. The marbles should fit together loosely.

2. Close the lid on the box.

3. Using both hands, lift the box and, while holding the lid secure, shake the box vigorously up and down, then side to side.

4. Quickly set the box on a table.

5. Open the lid and observe the position of the marbles inside.

Results

Shaking the box moves the marbles, leaving them in a disorderly arrangement.

Why?

As the temperature of liquid rock within the earth increases, the movement of the molecules in the rock increases. The movement of magma molecules is symbolized in this experiment by the movement of the marbles as the box is shaken. During volcanic eruptions, liquid rock reaches the earth's surface and cools quickly in a matter of days or even hours. This rapid cooling of lava means that the molecules don't have time to move into orderly patterns before the rock solidifies. This produces igneous rock. (*Igneous* is a Latin word meaning "fire.") If the rock is formed by the solidification of lava poured out onto the earth's surface, it is called an **extrusive igneous rock**.

The irregular organization of molecules in extrusive rocks results in rocks with small crystals or no crystals. This occurs because the molecules in the liquid rock cooled so quickly that only a few or none at all had time to move into an orderly crystalline position. Extrusive igneous rocks with small crystals, such as in basalt, are described as fine-grained, and those with no crystals, such as obsidian, are described as glassy.

LET'S EXPLORE

Would slow, gentle shaking over a longer period affect the results? Repeat the experiment, but after shaking, place the box on a table and very gently vibrate the box back and forth and from side to side for about 15 seconds. The resulting orderly, single layer of marbles represents the crystalline structure of **intrusive igneous rocks** (igneous rock formed by the slow cooling of magma below the earth's surface).

SHOW TIME!

1. Specimens of igneous rocks can be collected or purchased at a rock shop. Examine the samples with a magnifying lens, and sort the rocks into groups labeled INTRUSIVE and EXTRUSIVE. Include the name, texture, and mineral content of each rock as part of this display.

INTRUSIVE   EXTRUSIVE

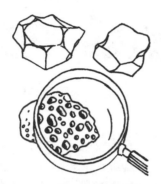

2. The difference in crystal size in igneous rocks is due to the rate at which the liquid rock cools. Demonstrate this by asking an adult to make fudge using the following recipe and separating the mixture into two batches; one will cool slowly, forming larger, intrusive crystals, and the other will cool quickly, forming smaller, extrusive crystals.

Fudge

In a pot, combine ¾ cup (188 ml) of cocoa, 3 cups (750 ml) granulated sugar, and 1½ cups (375 ml) milk. Cook slowly until the chocolate is thoroughly blended, stirring gently. Boil while stirring to 234° Fahrenheit (112° C) or until the mixture forms a soft ball when dropped into cold water. Remove the pot from the heat, and add 1 teaspoon (5 ml) of vanilla extract and 2 tablespoons (30 ml) of margarine. Stir thoroughly. Pour 5 tablespoons (75 ml) of the mixture onto a sheet of aluminum foil. Immediately fold the edges of the foil together to seal the foil around the hot mixture. Vigorously beat the remaining mixture until it is thick and has a shiny appearance. Then pour it onto a buttered plate. Taste the two batches of fudge after they have cooled to room temperature. The intrusive candy will taste grainy while the extrusive candy will taste smooth.

CHECK IT OUT!

Basalt, andesite, and rhyolite basalt are the three types of fine-grained extrusive rocks. Scoria and pumice are types of glassy extrusive rocks. Find out more about igneous rocks. How are scoria and pumice formed? What are the common intrusive rocks and which is the most abundant? Why do rocks of the same composition sometimes have different-sized crystals?

![Volcano illustration] **18**

Before and After

PROBLEM

How do streams and rivers behave before and after a volcanic explosion?

Materials

scissors
ruler
heavyweight aluminum foil
cookie sheet
pencil
3-ounce (90-ml) paper cup
marble
tap water
book

Procedure

1. Cut a 10-inch × 10-inch (25-cm × 25-cm) piece of aluminum foil.

2. Fold the piece in half, lengthwise, twice, forming a strip 10 inches × 2.5 inches (25 cm × 6.25 cm).

3. Six inches (15 cm) from one end of the strip, cut ¾-inch (1.9-cm) slits on both edges.

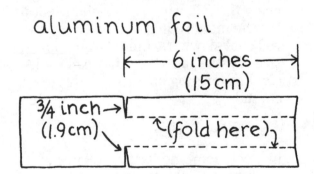

aluminum foil

|← 6 inches →|
(15 cm)

¾ inch →
(1.9 cm)

↖(fold here)↘

4. Bend the sides of the 6-inch (15-cm) section upward.

5. Raise the 4-inch (10-cm) end of the foil and bend it down over the edge of the cookie sheet to create a ramp.

6. Position a marble at the end of the channel formed by the aluminum foil.

7. Use the point of the pencil to punch a small hole in the side of the paper cup just above its bottom edge.

8. Place your finger over the hole in the cup, and fill the cup with tap water.

9. Use the book to support the cup on the top edge of the cookie sheet, with the hole in the cup pointing toward the channel.

10. Remove your finger and allow the water to flow out of the hole in the cup.

11. Observe any movement of the marble as the water flows down and out of the channel.

Results

The water pouring out the small hole slowly moves down the channel, around the marble, and out into the cookie sheet. The marble is affected only slightly, or not at all, by the small stream of flowing water.

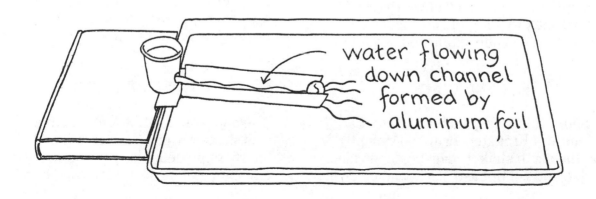

water flowing down channel formed by aluminum foil

Why?

The small amount of water flowing down the paper channel does not have enough force to push the marble out of its way. The water hits the marble and is redirected around its sides. The small amount of water simulates the gentle flow of clear water from rainfall and slow-melting snow down the slope of an inactive volcano.

LET'S EXPLORE

What would happen if a larger amount of water was released from the cup? Repeat the original experiment, replacing the cup with a cup that has a hole slightly larger than the diameter of the pencil. The water released from this cup represents the massive water flow produced by the quick melting of snow and ice by heat from a volcanic explosion.

SHOW TIME!

Some volcanoes, such as Mount St. Helens and Krakatoa, erupt so violently that the earth shakes, causing landslides. Dark clouds of hot ash, rock, and dirt can be blasted upward from the vent for many miles. Mudflows can form by the mixing of fast-melting snow and ice with the ash, rock, and dirt that rain down onto the slopes. Demonstrate the formation of mudflows by performing the following outdoor activity:

- Lay a cookie sheet on the ground and raise one end about 2 inches (5 cm) by putting soil under the edge of the sheet.

- Cover the sheet with a layer of soil.

- Fill a 1-gallon (4-liter) jug with tap water.

- Tilt the water jug so that its mouth is about 6 inches (15 cm) from the raised end of the cookie sheet. Photographs taken before and after the water is poured onto the soil can be used as project displays.

CHECK IT OUT!

1. The appearance of Mount St. Helens was strikingly different before and after it exploded, blowing about one cubic mile of its northern slope into

the air. Find out more about the geological changes in the rivers and streams caused by Mount St. Helens' eruption on May 18, 1980. How long did the mudflows and flood waters last? Were all the changes in the streams and rivers permanent?

2. Many volcanoes erupt each year on earth. Mudflows are one kind of hazard that threaten the lives of the millions of people that live near volcanoes. Find out more about the hazards created by volcanic eruptions, such as *lateral blasts* that can overwhelm people before they can flee, violent undersea eruptions that cause sea waves, poisonous gases that can suffocate, and hot ash that can bury people.

19

Block Out

PROBLEM

How can volcanic clouds lower atmo-spheric temperature?

Materials

white poster board
outdoor table (optional)
scissors
ruler
clear, plastic report cover
8 paper cups
8-inch × 10-inch (20-cm × 25-cm) piece
   of cardboard
2 thermometers
timer

Procedure

NOTE: This activity must be performed outdoors on a sunny day.

1. Lay the poster board on the table or on the ground.

2. Cut a single 8-inch × 10-inch (20-cm × 25-cm) piece from the report cover.

3. Set four of the paper cups, upside down, on the poster board. Space them so that one cup sits under each corner of the plastic sheet, which should sit on top.

4. Position the remaining four paper cups on the poster board in a similar manner, so that the bottom of each cup sits under each corner of the piece of cardboard.

5. Read and record the temperature on both thermometers.

6. Place one thermometer on the poster board under the plastic sheet and the

other thermometer under the cardboard. *NOTE: It is best to perform this experiment at midday so that the sun's rays shine directly onto the materials.*

7. After 15 minutes, read and record the temperature on both thermometers.

Results

The thermometer under the clear plastic sheet has a higher temperature than the one under the cardboard.

Why?

The clear plastic sheet is **transparent**, which means it allows the sun's light to pass through. The cardboard does not allow light to pass through, making it an **opaque** object. Normally, the atmosphere of the earth is relatively transparent. The clouds formed by some volcanic eruptions contain opaque ash particles that block out some of the sun's solar rays. This results in a lowering of atmospheric temperature, just as the opaque cardboard blocking the sun's rays resulted in a lower temperature on the thermometer underneath it.

LET'S EXPLORE

How would particles less opaque than volcanic ash, such as gas, affect the atmospheric temperature? Repeat the experiment, replacing the cardboard with a blue transparent sheet of plastic.

SHOW TIME!

1. In June 1783, Laki Volcano in Iceland erupted. This eruption did not produce a dense cloud of debris, but for months large amounts of gas poured out into the atmosphere. The concentration of this gas in the air resulted in a bluish haze that covered the sky and ruined crops. The volcanic haze from the Laki eruption can be demonstrated by covering the opening of a flashlight with opaque paper that has a hole in the center; this allows a small beam of light to pass through. Fill a glass with water, add one drop of milk to the water, and stir. In a darkened room, direct the beam of light through the solution. The contents of the glass will look hazy.

2. The combination of reduced sunlight resulting from a thick blanket of volcanic debris and huge amounts of toxic gases released from volcanoes destroys crops. Plants need the sun for

an energy-producing reaction called photosynthesis. **Photosynthesis** is the process by which plants use light energy, carbon dioxide, and water to produce their own food. Demonstrate the affect of reduced sunlight on crops by putting potted plants inside boxes with open tops. Cover each box with a different colored plastic sheet or a piece of cardboard. Check the plants once a day for two weeks. Photographs of the daily development of the plants can be displayed.

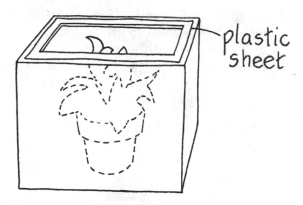

plastic sheet

CHECK IT OUT!

1. The largest volcanic eruption in recorded history occurred in April of 1815. Tambora Volcano in Indonesia's Lesser Sunda Islands exploded, sending a towering dense cloud into the atmosphere. Find out more about this and other violent volcanic eruptions that produced thick clouds of ash and gas. Was Benjamin Franklin the first person to determine that volcanic eruptions could affect climate? How can one volcano affect global climate? Do volcanic clouds always lower atmospheric temperatures? What is the *greenhouse effect*? What is the *global warming effect*?

2. Ash from volcanoes such as Laki can produce months of hazy skies. They also produce brilliant and colorful sunrises and sunsets. These changes in the color of the sky are due to refraction of light. Find out more about how volcanic eruptions cause changes in the color of the atmosphere. Use a physical science text to find out more about light refraction. Another source of information is "Blue Sky," page 28 in *Astronomy for Every Kid* (New York: Wiley, 1991), by Janice VanCleave.

20

Sinker

PROBLEM

How is a volcanic caldera formed?

Materials

scissors
ruler
poster board
2-liter soda bottle
2 cups (500 ml) of soil
large bowl
tap water
teaspoon (5-ml spoon)
adult helper

Procedure

1. Cut two 3-inch × 8-inch (7.5-cm × 20-cm) strips of poster board.

2. Ask an adult helper to cut the top from the soda bottle.

3. Ask your helper to cut two horizontal slits, one on each side in the center of the bottle and large enough for the poster-board strips to slide through.

4. Pour the soil into the bowl and add water, 1 teaspoon (5 ml) at a time, while mixing with your hands. Continue adding the water until the soil is slightly moist and begins to stick together.

5. Place half of the moist soil inside the bottle.

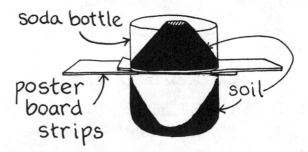

soda bottle

poster board strips

soil

6. Press the soil against the sides of the bottle up to the slits, leaving a large, empty cavity in the center.

7. Place the strips of poster board, one on top of the other, through the slits in the bottle.

8. Place the remaining soil on top of the strips of poster board and mold it into the shape of a volcano top, as shown in the diagram.

9. Hold the ends of the strips, one in each hand, and slowly pull the strips in opposite directions.

10. Observe the top of the volcano as the strips separate.

Results

When the supporting strips are removed, the top of the volcano falls into the cavity below.

Why?

The soil falling into the cavity below simulates the formation of a volcanic **caldera** (a large, roughly circular crater with steep walls formed when the top of a volcano collapses). The rapid ejection of magma during a large volcanic eruption can leave the magma chamber empty or partially empty. The unsupported roof of the empty chamber can slowly sink under its own weight, forming a caldera.

LET'S EXPLORE

1. Would the size of the cavity affect the results? Repeat the original experiment using twice as much soil inside the bottle.

2. Does the size of the volcano above the cavity affect the results? Repeat the original experiment using two cups of soil to build the volcano on top of the paper strips.

SHOW TIME!

1. Before the Pioneer-Venus space craft began its orbit around Venus in 1978, only a limited amount of information was known about the planet. The craft had many instruments, but its **radar altimeter** (the instrument that uses echo signals to determine profile of a land surface) allowed scientists to peek through the thick blanket of clouds that covers the planet in order to collect information about its surface. The altimeter readings revealed that Venus has lowlands, rolling plains, and highlands. In the highlands, the readings indicate possible volcanoic structures similar to **shield volcanoes** (volcanoes composed of layers of solidified lava, a wide base, and a large, bowl-shaped opening at the top) on earth. There is some evidence of the presence of a caldera.

Simulate the use of a radar altimeter by placing small blocks of wood against a wall to represent land features with different altitudes (see diagram). Roll a small rubber ball along the floor and record the time it takes for the ball to return to you. The rolling and reflecting of the ball off the blocks of wood simulates the sending of radio signals from a radar altimeter and their return after bouncing off a surface.

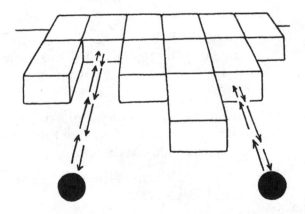

2. An interesting volcanic feature on the earth's moon is the presence of rilles. **Rilles** are long, straight or winding valleys cut in the surface. These channels may have formed by lava flowing on the surface or possibly by lava that flowed underground. When the lava drained away, the roof of the underground tunnel collapsed, forming a valley. This happens on earth, too, or anywhere there is volcanic action with lava flow. These underground tunnels are known as lava tubes.

You can demonstrate the development of rilles by filling a small box about three-fourths full with dry sand or salt.

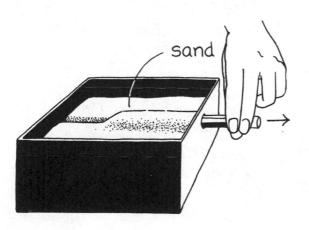

sand

Punch a hole in the side of the box and insert a pencil so that it lies flat on the surface of the sand. Sprinkle a thin layer of sand over the pencil. Slowly pull the pencil out of the hole. Photographs of the surface before and after removing the pencil can be displayed, along with pictures of the moon's surface showing the rilles.

CHECK IT OUT!

1. The formation of a caldera does not always indicate that the volcano will not become active again. Find out more about the formation of calderas and how the collapsed floor of the caldera can be lifted. What is a *resurgent dome*? How was Wizard Island formed in the middle of Crater Lake?

2. Some scientists believe that volcanoes on Venus are actively erupting right now. Find out more about the volcanoes on Venus and other celestial bodies in our solar system. Are there volcanoes on Mercury's smooth plains? Are there volcanoes beneath the thick atmosphere covering Saturn's largest satellite, Titan?

Glossary

Asthenosphere The portion of the mantle below the lithosphere.

Batholith Large mass of intrusive igneous rock extending to unknown depths.

Buoyant Able to float.

Caldera A large, roughly circular crater with steep walls formed when the top of a volcano collapses.

Composite volcano Cone-shaped volcano formed by alternating layers of solidified lava and rock particles.

Core The innermost, hottest layer of the earth; can be divided into the outer core and inner core.

Crater The bowl-shaped depression at the top of a volcano.

Crust The relatively thin, outermost, coolest layer of the earth.

Density The scientific way of comparing the "heaviness" of materials. It is a measurement of the mass of a specific volume.

Dike Narrow, vertical intrusion that rises and breaks through horizontal rock layers.

Epicenter The point on the earth's surface directly above the focus of an earthquake.

Extensiometer Instrument used by volcanologists to measure changes in the diameter of a volcano.

Extrusive igneous rock Igneous rocks formed by the solidification of molten rock at or near the earth's surface; it is also known as extrusive rock.

Focus The underground point of origin of an earthquake.

Friction A force that acts against motion; this resistance to motion produces heat.

Fumaroles Volcanic vents from which only gas escapes.

Igneous rock Rock formed by the cooling and solidification of magma.

Immiscible liquids Liquids that are not able to mix together.

Inertia Resistance of an object to any change in motion; it stays still or continues to move in a straight line unless some force acts on it.

Insoluble Describes a substance that is incapable of being dissolved.

Intrusion Magma that cools and hardens before reaching the surface.

Intrusive igneous rock   Igneous rock formed by the slow cooling and solidification of magma below the earth's surface.

Intrusive volcanism   Movement of magma beneath the earth's surface.

Laccolith   Domed-shaped body of intrusive igneous rock that has pushed up the overlying rock layer.

Lava   Magma that has reached the earth's surface.

Lithosphere   The uppermost layer of the earth; includes all of the crust and the uppermost part of the mantle.

Magma   Molten rock material beneath the surface of the earth.

Magma chamber   A pool of magma deep within the earth.

Magnetometer   An instrument used to measure magnetic strength of a material.

Mantle   The second layer of the earth; hotter than the crust but cooler than the core.

Mid-ocean ridges   Where the crust of the earth is expanding.

Opaque   Describes a material that does not allow light to pass through it.

Optical pyrometer   An instrument used to measure the temperature of hot materials, such as hot lava flowing from a volcano.

Photosynthesis   The process by which plants use light energy, carbon dioxide, and water to make their own food.

Plasticity   The ability of a solid material to flow.

Plate tectonic theory   Explanation of the movement of earth's crust; states that the crust is made of moving plates that float on hot liquid.

Pumice   Volcanic rock formed when large amounts of volcanic gases mix with a viscous magma.

Radar altimeter   An instrument that uses echo signals to determine the profile of land surfaces.

Radioactive decay   A breaking apart of the nucleus of an atom; this change produces heat.

Rilles   Long, straight or winding valleys cut in the surface of celestial bodies by above- or below-ground lava flows.

Seismogram   A printed record made by a seismometer.

Seismometer   An instrument used to measure the shaking energy of an earthquake.

Shield volcano   A volcano composed of layers of solidified lava, a wide base, and a large, bowl-shaped opening at the top.

Sill   Thin, horizontal sheet of intrusive igneous rock sandwiched between other rock layers.

Stock   Mass of intrusive igneous rock, similar but smaller than batholith bodies.

Stoping   The process by which blocks of solid rock in the path of magma are broken, melted, and added to the flowing, hot, liquid rock.

Tiltmeter   An instrument that measures the amount of tilt of the ground on the sides of a volcano, caused by magma and gases pushing the ground upward.

Transparent   Describes a material that allows light to pass through it.

Vent   Channel of a volcano that connects the source of magma to the volcano's opening.

Viscometer   Meter used to measure the flow rate of a fluid.

Viscosity   The measurement of a liquid's ability to flow.

Volcano   Opening in the earth's crust from which molten rock, steam, ash, and rock fragments are expelled.

Volcanologist   A scientist who studies volcanoes.

Index

seismometer, 56–59
  definition of, 58
  construction of, 56–58
shield volcano, 82
Sierra Nevada Mountains, 63
sills, 63
stocks, 63
stoping, 15
stratovolcano, 39
Tambora Volcano, 79
tiltmeter, 48–51
vent, 17, 38
viscometer, 64–67
viscosity:
  definition of, 19, 66
  of magma, 64–67
volcano:
  effect on atmosphere, 76–79
  belts, 35
  cones, 22
  definition of, 7
  diameter changes of, 52–55
  eruption predictions, 40–55
  eruption types, 31, 38
  gases in, 24–30, 44–47
  Krakatoa, 31

Laki Volcano, 78
location of, 32–35
magnetic field of, 40–42
models of, 20–23
Mount Pinatubo, 31
Mount St. Helens, 31
effect on rivers and streams, 72–75
side vents of, 38
Tambora Volcano, 79
types, 36–39, 82
volcanologists, 41, 54, 59

More Exciting and Fun Activity Books from Janice VanCleave . . .
Available from your local bookstore or simply use the order form below.

Mail to: Jennifer Bergman, John Wiley and Sons, Inc., 605 Third Avenue, New York, New York, 10158-0012

Title	ISBN	Price
__ ANIMALS	55052-3	$9.95
__ EARTHQUAKES	57107-5	$9.95
__ ELECTRICITY	31010-7	$9.95
__ GRAVITY	55050-7	$9.95
__ MACHINES	57108-3	$9.95
__ MAGNETS	57106-7	$9.95
__ MICROSCOPES	58956-X	$9.95
__ MOLECULES	55054-X	$9.95
__ VOLCANOES	30811-0	$9.95
__ ASTRONOMY	53573-7	$10.95
__ BIOLOGY	50381-9	$10.95
__ CHEMISTRY	62085-8	$10.95
__ DINOSAURS	30812-9	$10.95
__ EARTH SCIENCE	53010-7	$10.95
__ GEOGRAPHY	59842-9	$10.95
__ GEOMETRY	31141-3	$10.95
__ MATH	54265-2	$10.95
__ PHYSICS	52505-7	$10.95
__ 200 GOOEY, SLIPPERY, SLIMY, WEIRD, & FUN EXPERIMENTS		
	57921-1	$12.95
__ 201 AWESOME, MAGICAL, BIZARRE, & INCREDIBLE EXPERIMENTS		
	31011-5	$12.95

TOTAL: _____

To Order
by Phone:

Call
1-800-225-5945

[ ] Check/Money Order Enclosed
[ ] Charge my ___ Visa ___ Mastercard ___AMEX ___Discover
Card # _____Exp. Date _____
(Wiley pays postage & handling on all prepaid orders)

NAME:_____

ADDRESS:_____

CITY:_____ STATE:_____ ZIP:_____

SIGNATURE:_____ (Offer Not Valid Unless Signed)

WILEY
Publishers Since 1807